Balance Is Bullshit

A Solopreneurs Guide To Making Fucking Decisions That Matter

Balance Is BULLSHIT

A Solopreneurs Guide To Making Fucking Decisions That Matter

Phyllis Williams-Strawder

Copyright © 2022 Phyllis Williams-Strawder

Balance Is Bullshit
Phyllis Williams-Strawder

Published 2022, by Espresso Mischief Publishing
hello@espressomischief.com
Galveston, TX 77551 USA

Paperback ISBN: 978-1-7330957-7-8

Library of Congress Control Number: 2022915796

All rights reserved. No part of this publication may be reproduced, distributed or transmitted in any form or by any means, including photocopying, recording, or other electronic or mechanical methods, without the prior written permission of the publisher, except in the case of brief quotations embodied in critical reviews and certain other noncommercial uses permitted by copyright law.

Printed in the United States of America

Front Cover Illustration by Daniel Cady

Dedication

This is dedicated to the clients who became fam and the fam who became clients.

Cas - Ebony - Shawna - Tametra

They have made me exponentially better than I could have been by myself.

TABLE OF CONTENTS

Introduction 1

- PART I -
How Do You See Your Life 6

- PART II -
Balance Is Bullshit 11
Damn Distractions 16
Struggle Juggles 22
Facing Flaws 27

- PART III -
Family & Social Relationships 34
    Relationship Evaluation 36
    Relationship Truths 37
    Relationship Decision 38
Business & Education Aspirations 39
    Business & Education Evaluation 40
    Business & Education Truths 41
    Business & Education Decision 42
Financial Relationship 43
    Financial Relationship Evaluation 44
    Financial Relationship Truths 45
    Financial Relationship Decision 46

Health, Recreation, & Leisure 47
   Health, Recreation & Leisure Evaluation 48
   Health, Recreation & Leisure Truths 49
   Health, Recreation & Leisure Decision 50
Routine Responsibilities 51
   Routine Responsibilities Evaluation 52
   Routine Responsibilities Truths 53
   Routine Responsibilities Decision 54
Contribution & Giving Back 55
   Contribution & Giving Back Evaluation 56
   Contribution & Giving Back Truths 57
   Contributing & Giving Back Decision 58
Mental, Emotional, & Spiritual 59
   Mental, Emotional & Spiritual Evaluation 60
   Mental, Emotional & Spiritual Truths 61
   Mental, Emotional & Spiritual Decisions 62

- PART III -

Wrap It Up 64
No Pressure 71
Other Books By The Author 75
About the Author 76

Introduction

Being a solopreneur is some exciting and scary shit. It's the independence you always wanted in a career, but without the safety net of 401k's and sick days. What the FUCK were you thinking?

Evidently you're the type who doesn't scare easy and I like that. You're not afraid of a challenge. The solopreneur challenge you face everyday is juggling all the roles you fill. Gone are the days of clocking in and scheduled lunches. You've replaced it with the excitement and the drive of doing it how you want. And you want it all. NOW!

The previous version of this book was titled, <u>Finding Life Balance</u>, but in case you didn't get the memo, balance is bullshit. Life is lived, not balanced. There is no cosmic scale where all things are even.

When you drank the kool-aid of entrepreneurship, you weren't seeking balance. You signed on for the juggle. You didn't know that until you made the leap that there are a million and one decisions you have to make. It's those decisions that try to pull your focus in different directions at the same time. Your attempt to look everywhere at once will empty your soul. Pouring from an empty soul is not what life is about.

Let's start with everyone's biggie, finances. If you're a bootstrapping solopreneur, using up all your finances can quickly drive you into debt. Because you're a business of one, you begin to see every relationship as a means to a sale. All the joy and fun you used to have seems to take a back seat to the business. It's not intentional. It's the anxious excitement of making it work.

Living a solopreneur lifestyle requires a series of choices. You may think they're complicated, but they're as simple as yes or no. When you say yes to one thing, you say no to something else. Some will say it's not that cut and dry, but it truly is. It's when you feel the need to justify the yes or no to others that it gets complicated.

Shying away from decision-making comes in various forms with lots of questions. What if they get mad? What if they don't like me or it? And here's the biggie. WHAT IF I GET IT WRONG?

In your mind, getting it wrong feels as if it will be the death of you every time. Check your pulse right now. That's right. You're still here. You learned. You adapted or adjusted. You kept it push'n. I really hate the saying, BUT done is better than perfect, but getting it done is a fucking decision.

How you make decisions in your life, brand, and business is how you juggle. Yes, decision making is the least attractive thing about business when you're still learning your business. It goes back to the yes/no dichotomy. When you have a job most of the yes/no decisions are made for you. In your new role as a solopreneur, the buck stops with you until you grow, scale and give someone else some of the yes/no responsibility.

Our restaurant back in the day was named after my husband, "Bigmista." I would often remind him that at the end of the day, all final decisions fell to him because his name was on the door. Looking back I recognize that as a bitch move. I can only imagine the pressure I was putting on him. I know it came from a selfish place. Being in the restaurant business was not my dream even though it was my idea. But that's a story for another time.

Working together and living together was never balanced for us. It took years to figure out how to make it work. I actually came up with what I called my S.A.N.I.T.Y. method because I was the one who created most of the problems of our unbalanced lives.

In those days I was known as Mrs. Mista to his Bigmista and I seldom turned her off. My husband would go to bed with Mrs. Mista and her laptop. Later, he would hear my wife voice at the shop. My daughter should have called me "5 more minutes" instead of mom. I was that bad. And my mom was constantly hinting at me being a bad mom for not spending more time with my daughter.

My juggling game was shit back then and I wasn't even a solo act. But, over the years of building what I then called a bbq empire, I learned to make better decisions about my life, brand, and business. The best decision was to set boundaries, not try to achieve balance. Now I know better, so I do better and so will you.

- PART I -

How Do You See Your Life

Let's kick this shit off with getting some real answers to your life as a solopreneur. Have you been rock'n the business leader role for a while? Do you think you shoulda exchanged the solo for an entre by now? Do you have the life you think you should have by being your own boss?

Am I pissing you off by asking? If I am it's because you see your life in a less than flattering way. The questions weren't accusatory, but you answered them as if they were.

When you're young, you dream dreams. What celebrity you'll marry. How big your mansion will be. The house you'll buy for your mom. When you start a business you have different dreams. No one will boss you around anymore. You don't have to punch a clock. You get to make all the money. So what's the up? I'll share a couple of mine so you don't have to go first.

I went all the way back to the schoolyard for this one. I allowed childhood bullying to control my adult decisions. Damn near every chance I wanted to take in life and business got filtered through the eyes of a child who didn't wanna be noticed.

Attempting to hide behind the awkward kid I was wasn't easy. I'm a 6'1", not so small (since I married my husband) big personality, woman. In familiar company I was cool. In business, I would seek the advice of the girl I was to see if we were scared. We usually were. This is so not how I saw my life.

Trying not to be noticed as a business person is an oxymoron for sure. When feelings trump logic, that's what happens. You push yourself to the background

Another hold up for me was being taught to dream small. I found out small dreams come from well-meaning people with "good advice." You know what I'm talking about.

"Ooh, baby. Get an education. This field pays a lot of money. Do what I did. Save up for retirement."

Just typing this makes my soul cringe. I know killing dreams with *good advice* is not intentional. It's a byproduct. You take it and try to make it work *or* you feel guilty for wanting to live a dream of your own. Either way, you bear the weight of someone else's expectations. What you're left with is someone else telling you what you're worth under the label of competitive salary with little to no room for you to ask for more.

How you see your life is subjective. It's a paradigm thing. You can live in the same house with someone from birth and have different world views. You may have the same hold up as someone else but the view is different through their eyes. Now I want you to put on your grown up draws, look at your life objectively, and answer some questions as honestly as possible.

Q1) Summarize what your ideal life would be like.
___
___
___

Q2) What are the main challenges or difficulties you face in having that life?
___
___
___

Q3) What challenges or difficulties are you ready to deal with so you can have that life?
___
___
___

Q4) What challenges or difficulties are you not ready to deal with so you can have that life?
___
___
___

Q5) What challenges or difficulties are you going to deal with so you can have that life?
___
___
___

- PART II -

Balance Is Bullshit

Trying to live a balanced life is the ultimate unicorn rainbow bullshit. It's fantasy thinking at its finest. Balance by definition means all things have equal weight or value. In life that means EVERYTHING gets equal attention. If anyone has that type of life, then they are a fictional character or a delusional, lying ass.

There are 24 hours in a day. They cannot be spaced evenly to fit everything you do in your life, brand and business as a solopreneur. IJS.

Imagine you're in a world where you have six, just six, balls to juggle on the regular: significant other, extended family, business, money, sleep, eat. These are the balls you chose to juggle with. Each one needs your undivided attention for four hours every day. Yes; I'm that damn literal and the dictionary agrees with me. Balance is "a state of equilibrium; equal distribution of weight." To say balance is anything else is to say life is fair, but we all know what a crock of crap that is.

I never bought into this unicorn crazy of work/life balance. That's because it's nothing more than a person not wanting to spend most of their day (and over half their life) making somebody else rich. They also don't wanna live off the leftovers of their life.

I whole-heartedly agree that we spend too much time working. I object to defining a well-lived life as balance.

Play more, work less. Hmm? Let's see if the math works. You have full time job that takes up 8.5-9 hours per day. I won't count the commute and I will discount lunch. That's eight hours gone right there. As a solopreneur still figuring it out, for shits and giggles, let's make that ten hours.

As a healthy adult, you should get at least seven hours of sleep. Add that to your working hours and 15-17 of your 24 are gone. You have 7-9 hours left in which to live your best life. Please tell me when in the fresh hell the balance is supposed to kick in?

What it really boils down to is that you wanna do what you wanna do when you wanna do it. You're not seeking balance. You want a choice. When you make choices, it requires more of a juggling quality, not a balancing act. Life is life and it should work for you with as little guilt as possible from your mom.

Working is a part of life. It can be fun, fulfilling, or frustrating. How you choose to look at it is all that matters. If my husband came in here right now and said, "Close up that lap top and let's go." I can choose giggly girl and say, "Alright now Big Daddy." Or I can choose to continue writing.

* * *

Dammit, he didn't whisk me away, but give me a minute while I wipe the grin off my face.

* * *

> *"There's no such thing as work-life balance. There are work-life choices, and you make them, and they have consequences."*
>
> *- Jack Welch*

Therein lies the juggle. Dropping my work for my husband. No more. No less. A decision. The exciting never-ending juggling of what you need or want at any given moment.

You juggle and jostle your life around until it makes sense to you and those you care about. You can choose to pick up what falls or say fuck it and walk away. As a solopreneur every day is a juggle between choosing to or not. On busy days it can feel like everything is a series of *get in where you fit in* moments.

If you feel like you made a wrong choice, it can throw off how you juggle. Saying things like, "This is gonna mess up my whole day," is you making a choice to live your day messed up. Living under that cloud of Murphy's Law is you making a choice that wrong things are meant to happen.

If you think you can get away with not making a choice, think again. Doing nothing is a choice that get's you nothing.

You are gonna have fucked up days. The beauty is choosing how long you will sit with it. There is no balance in that choice. You can wallow or you can keep it push'n. I relish an occasional pity party or moment of pettiness though. IJS.

I found choosing to wallow too long has a tendency to distract you from a solution. You'll focus on others around you and what you deem their successes. You wonder why they're crushing it and you're in the ninth circle of hell.

In this tech age, most of what you're looking at is a social media facade. Contrary to what some folx do in your timeline, social media is not meant to air your dirty laundry, especially when you have a business. You don't have to be so transparent that you share all your fuck ups. But you can be vulnerable enough to admit that life is not perfect.

I realize juggling is a life long pursuit. Knowing that everything in life is not a flaming ball of crazy makes it easier. Choose to pick up things that don't bear the weight of the world.

Traffic is traffic; not God trying to make you late for a meeting. Spilled coffee is coffee; not the fashion police asking why did you wear that today. They are annoyances and inconvenient. So catch the words before they leave your lips as a careless thought, "Oh Lord, it's gonna be one of those days."

Saying things like that is like you throwing all your balls in the air and saying fuck it. I'm done. You put into motion an avalanche that will make it feel like your day is going down in flames. If you choose to see the rest of the day that way, every ball you go to pick up will feel like a flaming turd. Not a pretty image, right?

Damn Distractions

Distractions are amazing procrastination tools for not growing your business. In your head you're doing everything you can to make your business work but nothing's happening. I remember mentally exhausting myself for days with long work hours because distractions had gotten the better of me.

A distraction you may not recognize is disguised as work. It makes you think you're busy. The reality is you are distracting yourself from a tough business decision.

The more you turn to this type of distraction, the more you jeopardize your business. I call it work tweaking. The reason it's so dangerous is because you actually think you're getting shit done.

Distracted work looks like a website that's never quite right. Then there's the look and vibe of your email sequence. That's followed by never knowing. There are classes, conferences, trainings and workshops to keep you distracted.

Money and marketing are usually the culprits behind these distractions. You spend $97 to take an online course to make a million dollars. Then you spend another $97 on Facebook ads to make that million dollars.

Two things wrong with this foolishness: the first thing is if you could make a million dollars from a $97 investment, no one would be broke. The second thing is trying to market what you learned for $97 and get paid more than $970. Yes, it's a big ass exaggeration. No, it's not uncommon.

This fuckery is predicated on the new thinking of getting rich from being one step ahead of your audience. When it doesn't work, you get distracted by guru and celebrity advice.

I don't wanna hurt your feelings tOo much so let's talk about the other time suck distractions of a solopreneur.

When I wrote the first edition of this book, I spent days writing and rewriting til 4AM because of distractions. What I should have done was take my ass

Balance Is Bullshit

to bed so I could reset. That way when 7AM ticked up on my ass, I would be ready for my homeschool mom close up. Yes, I SUUUCKED at not being distracted. I did not want my daughter to suffer the same fate.

For full disclosure, my out of control juggling started long before my solopreneur days. I have ample proof with my journal fetish and writing only on the first few pages. I would often have what I thought were great ideas. So I would try to fit them into my day because I convinced myself everything had to get done.

> *"I intentionally abandoned the hard stuff early on because not only do I think it's useless, I think it's a distraction."*
> - Seth Godin

I pushed myself from juggling distractions to procrastination to anxiety. I would distract myself from the anxiety by being a martyr for the cause of women who can do it all. Playing games all fucking day was disguised as a guilty pleasure.

Fear of not making enough drove me. I had to have multiple irons in the fire in case one failed. Truth was, all my shit was raggedy including my marriage and parenting. It never occurred to me to stop adding shit to an already full life. I wanted to live up to the standard of those women who said I could do it all. That's crazy talk and anyone trying to tell me different TA-DAY is looking for a fight.

See, I was that extra kinda special because I added distractions to my distractions. First, I diagnosed myself with OCD. I don't even really know what OCD is, but whatever. Second, I worked my mind around the premises that anything I did should start or end on a quarter hour mark. So if I was in the middle of something, AND I missed starting or stopping on a quarter hour mark, I would keep going and try to make the next one. I could easily spend 2-3 hours with this foolishness. And that's not the worse of it.

Man o man, the game apps. Back then mine was Candy Crush or some form of bubble pop game. I would tell myself to finish three levels by the time the clock hit a quarter mark then get back to work. If I wasn't paying attention or in the middle of a level and missed it, I would keep going until the next quarter hour mark. Oh, but if I had a couple of minutes left, I would start a new level knowing it would make me go over.

In my *bass-ackward* mind I had a point to prove. I had to reach my goal. I had to do it by a certain time. And I had to do it without using or buying any extras. By my law of distraction, I could make it up when everyone else was asleep.

The usual events of making up time were my husband waking in the middle of the night to find me missing. Best case scenario is him getting out of bed to find me by the glow of my laptop or iPad. Worse case scenario was him in bed next to me awaken by my keyboard tapping. In or out of bed, it was always the same question. "Why are you still up?" And it was usually the same answer. "I just wanna finish this."

Making up time was not confined to late night working. Oh, no. I raced against the estimated time of Google and Apple Maps. I know I'm not the only one. I sacrificed time with friends. On one side, I felt busy and important telling them I didn't have time. On the other end I felt frazzled and fake.

The lose/lose, however, was repeatedly telling my daughter, "Give me five more minutes." There's no getting that time back no matter how fast I drive. They were just efforts to justify my yes/no dichotomy.

Distractions have their place in how you live as a solopreneur. When you choose to use them as a means of escape the hard stuff, you're doing yourself and your business a disservice.

When you try to make up for it later on is when things get really bad and you spiral. You increase feelings of guilt and anxiety.

The deep down truth for me was I didn't know what the fuck I was doing. I didn't know how to fix it. I didn't know who or how to ask for help. It was easier to procrastinate with distractions and busy work than admit that.

It gnawed at me how jacked up my life was and I was making it worse. Unfortunately, knowing and gnawing wasn't enough to spur me into change. The fact that something could always wait, wasn't good enough for me. I hadn't let go of my mantra of you don't work, you don't eat. I couldn't sleep with that shit swirling around in my head.

It's more of a testament to my stubbornness than anything else. I meditated on my obsessive behavior and knew I had to make a choice. Ah, but wait, I was already making choices. I made a choice in how I invested (wasted) my time. I made a choice in where I invested (wasted) my time. I made a choice with whom I invested (wasted) my time. A choice is still a choice.

Your life as a solopreneur comes with its share of distractions. Giving in to them can cause you to feel some kinda way about making any choice. You need a good nights sleep. You need to have fun. You need to be around people.

Time is the one thing you can't get back or make more of. Sorry, my mom just spilled onto the page.

Struggle Juggles

The worst time to juggle decisions is when you're emotional. You throw rational thought out the window because being petty or childish at the moment feels so good. Oh. Maybe that's just me. No matter. Emotional business decisions can make things worse and lead you to a struggle juggle.

I'm a strong empath. So much so that I will go through a whole emotional spectrum with a stranger. Are we beat'n somebody up or are we gonna cry it out? I fall for sob stories and bullshit because I feel the pain of what they are going through. It's my struggle because being empathic don't pay the bills or wash the dishes.

The struggle juggle comes in many shapes and sizes. Juggling things that are too heavy for you will weigh you down. Juggling little things that don't matter will keep them slipping through your fingers. Juggling shit that ain't none a yo business is a waste. Life is beautiful and complex and challenging enough. You don't need to take on heavy stuff before you're ready or little stuff that don't mean nothing. You can definitely do without shit that has nothing to do with you.

> "The individual has always had to struggle to keep from being overwhelmed by the tribe. If you try it, you will be lonely often, and sometimes frightened. But no price is too high to pay for the privilege of owning yourself."
>
> - Rudyard Kipling

Falling into this cycle bleeds into your relationships because it stresses you the fuck out. You're angry because you're doing too much. You're doing too much because you're juggling the wrong things. Some of you are still juggling petty duties you should have delegated long ago. I don't care how much you know about multi-tasking and time management, you have a finite capacity.

You project your emotional stress and anxiety onto others. It comes from you not saying no to things that make you struggle. I don't promise you'll be stress and anxiety free if you say no, but you may enjoy your life more.

Yes, I speak from bad bitch experiences. Not the empathic bitch I am today. Back then, when and how you approached me during a struggle juggle never mattered. All I knew was that my time and space were invaded while I was putting out fires. My response to the invasion was never nice. Never mind that it was my bad choices that put me behind the eight ball. Whoever ventured close would reap the wrath of my frustration.

If you thrive under pressure then this may not be an issue for you. But if you are working under pressure because you wasted time, it's a different vibe. In my twisted world, spending time with friends and family felt like wasting time. Add the guilt of playing games for two hours when I could've worked increased the stress and struggle.

Here's a little secret I discovered about myself; if it's you too, you don't have to admit it out loud. Getting caught up in the struggle kept me busy. Being busy made me feel important and a little superior. Someone would ask, "Can you come out and play?"

"No. I'm busy. You know how it is."

There would be this little endorphin kick. In my head it sounded more like, "Yeah, bitches. Y'all got jobs. You wouldn't understand the life I've chosen. I'm a boss now and I don't have time for peasantry."

Just thinking about it makes me laugh out loud cause y'all know I'm telling the truth. You can be broke and busy and still pity the folx with traditional employment. It will pass. The struggle continues as you begin to look at the choices you made.

Me responding in bad bitch mode had everything to do with the choices I made. I saw them as a distraction that wasn't on the same level as Candy Crush and bubble pop games. Their distraction was unwanted. How batshit crazy is that?

I can't undo any of the choices I made. I can, however, learn from the struggles. If I didn't at least learn from them, then they are truly a waste. Justifying them is me wanting to feel better. Apologizing for them is me being hypocritical.

The choices you make are intentional even if the outcome is not. If they are not intentional that means your life has no rhyme or reason. You're choosing to take chances without considering the risk. You may as well throw all your darts at the board at the same time and hope one of them hits something good.

I was notorious for not apologizing. Instead I would say something like, "To hell with it, it's done now." Then I would round it out with a healthy dose of bullshit. That's when you vow to never allow yourself to behave like that again. I broke that vow. A LOT!

Closing your eyes to the choices that make you feel bad dooms you to repeat them. If your current state is a raggedy ass struggle juggle, look it in the face. You don't have to square off with it all the time. Somma my shit, I still can't look in the eye. That was denial. Trying to explain it away as, *"this is just how it is"* or *"they just have to deal with it"* is a cop out.

The easy answer to the struggle is learning to manage yourself and your time better. And to be clear, I said easy answer, not easy process. The back and forth of trying to fix yourself leads to more feelings of frustration and defeat. So what comes first, is facing what's going on in your life.

Facing Flaws

Plato said, "The first and best victory is to conquer self." In this tech life of games, notifications, and dopamine, it may feel like a moment to moment battle. If they are, then take the moment to moment victories. This is hard to do when you focus on the flaws and fuck ups instead of facing them.

Another great quote I like is from William Feather which says, "If we don't discipline ourselves, the world will do it for us."

Adding my own lived experience to Feather's words, I contend that not only will the world discipline you, it will humble you and knock you on your ass, if you're not careful.

For full transparency, I couldn't find where this quote originated. But everywhere I looked, it is credited to William Feather. I looked Feather up and now consider him a wise dude who knew his flaws and stumbling blocks. The various information I found sent me down rabbit holes. I came up confirming that looking at your life from the outside requires truth and grace.

Choosing to juggle a high-stress, busy, calendar-filled, solopreneur lifestyle doesn't work for long. At some point you can't be afraid to look behind the curtain to see who's really running Oz. Maybe it's the wizard who thinks you're juggling for the kids to have a better life. Maybe it's the wizard who thinks making all the money will solve all the problems. Ooh, maybe it's the wizard who's telling you to outrun your past.

> *"I've made peace with the fact that the things that I thought were weaknesses or flaws were just me. I like them."*
> - Sandra Bullock

Sweetheart, if the wizard is making you crazy, tell him to sit the fuck down. In case you're confused about which wizard is running you ragged, it don't matter. The wizard is holding a mirror and that's your reflection.

No one wants to face their flaws. They can show some ugly truth. They can also reveal some hidden gems. When you face them, you can no longer hide from who and what you are. That's some scary shit. That is until you realize it's not who you have to always be. Choices, baby. Choices.

So what now? Now is when you reflect some of that grace and forgiveness you give others on to yourself. You have the capacity to dish it out for everybody else until there's none left for you. You need something to shake you at your core in order to give yourself grace and forgiveness. You won't be able to see the things you can do something about until you do.

Hiding from what makes you, you can camouflage what makes you great. Instead you become a broke carbon copy of someone else's story. I can sometimes recognize the copy of a copy of a copy when folx try to fake the funk. You can't forgive yourself for not being that other person or the person someone else wanted you to be. That is wasted energy.

Wanting to hide is understandable when you have to juggle things like industry standards. It's a box of conformity by which success is measured. But, if you stop there you leave so much of your individual greatness off the table. Living up to someone else's standards outside of legal ramifications is stifling. It can crush your innovation outside of a corporate construct that will profit someone else financially.

Next you're asked to juggle trends. In this era of viral content, a trend could be over in a matter of days or hours. You have market and industry trends to contend with as well. Not keeping up with them can make you obsolete. So again, you hide because you measure your self-worth as a solopreneur by how trendy you are. If you don't catch it on the way up, how far behind are you really?

It's all a hot ass mess that distorts the image in the mirror. Yes, the struggle is real. Working through the struggle is hard. It's about getting better at choosing the right struggle for you, instead of making everything a struggle.

The evaluations in the next section cover seven key areas of your life. You juggle the choices of these areas every day. Use it to see what balls are missing from the mix. It's likely the areas causing you the most stress and frustration. If they're worth picking up, fine. If they're not, it's still fine. So just check in and see where you are with:

- *Family & Social Relationships*
- *Business & Education Aspirations*
- *Financial Relationships*

- *Health, Recreation & Leisure*
- *Life's Routine Responsibilities*
- *Giving Back & Contribution*
- *Mental, Emotional & Spiritual*

The importance placed on life areas is different for everyone. Most of you may run to the money. You think if you have enough, it will fix your other life areas. Let me burst that bubble for ya.

By saying money will fix everything, you're saying the rest of your life has no value. The better answer is to maintain an element of focus in all areas. This gives you a healthier life view and a healthier bank account.

Facing the areas of importance creates awareness of where improvement begins for YOU. You take steps toward a great life without letting so much good shit fall by the wayside. Overload happens when you try to give your all to everything because not only are you a solopreneur. You're one person.

Stepping into solopreneurship is as unique as your fingerprint. It is freedom personified. Yes, take good advice, just don't add it to the juggle if it makes you struggle.

Balance Is Bullshit

- PART III -

Family & Social Relationships

It can be easy to take for granted friends and family who support you on the regular as a solopreneur. You have this unspoken expectation that they should know and understand you're working to build an empire.

These things happen because you unknowingly look at your business from a selfish perspective. You unintentionally ignore the folx who show up for you everyday. You haphazardly push them to the background because you expect them to be there when YOU'RE ready.

It's not your fault. Everyone should see how hard you work and not take it personally. That's you placing blame instead of taking responsibility.

The saying that "we always hurt the ones we love" is a magnified truth for entrepreneurs. The anxiousness of being a business leader grips you. In their eyes you're acting out of character. And for a while that may be acceptable. But then you have to make a decision. Is this the new you or the momentary insanity of a person learning how to lead?

And it doesn't help to go to the extreme of denying yourself the joy of relationships, either. Casting love aside can leave an empty space that can't be filled by more work. Relationships make you whole and fill spaces for a reason, season, or lifetime. We were created to want to bond and relate and you should know where you currently stand in your relationships.

Take the evaluation. Be objective in your responses, but don't use them to make yourself feel bad. And don't look for excuses not to be honest. This is only for you.

If you're a loner type and friends and family aren't a priority right now, then acknowledge that and revisit it when you feel the need to. You get to decided when and with who you share your life with.

Balance Is Bullshit

Relationship Evaluation
On a scale of 1-10

___ How important are family relationships to you?
___ How important are social relationships to you?
___ How important are romantic relationships to you?

___ How satisfied are you with family relationships?
___ How satisfied are you with social relationships?
___ How satisfied are you with romantic relationships?

___ How healthy are your family relationships?
___ How healthy are your social relationships?
___ How healthy are your romantic relationships?

___ The people who matter the most in my life accept me.
___ I have close friendships with people I can be myself around.
___ I have a good social network/ am part of social groups.
___ I am generally good at connecting with new people.
___ How happy are you with the overall quality or your relationships?

Total Score ___

"There is no decision that we can make that doesn't come with some sort of balance or sacrifice." - Simon Sinek

Phyllis Williams-Strawder

Relationship Truths

Write down truths about your relationships that would benefit from your attention. These truths do not define you. They are just truths you're willing to face. Write about the relationships that are getting on your last damn nerve or the one you wish you had.

_____
_____
_____
_____
_____
_____
_____
_____
_____
_____
_____
_____
_____

Wounds from a friend can be trusted, but an enemy multiples kisses. - Prov 27:6

Relationship Decision

Turn your relationship truths into life decisions. You wrote about it, now be about it. Write if you're gonna do something about it or give it the finger. I won't tell.

I know…

_____

_____

_____

I want…

_____

_____

_____

I will…

_____

_____

_____

Business & Education Aspirations

There is nothing more liberating than taking off the limits of employment. That kind of freedom comes with a great deal of responsibility. If you go off the deep end, that freedom can feel like a prison.

Juggling decisions that determine your income and education was easy when someone told you what degree you needed and how much it was worth to them. The thing to hold on to is that even though you're a solopreneur you don't have to know everything and you can't make all the money.

Set realistic boundaries and expectations for your aspirations.

Business & Education Evaluation
On a scale of 1-10

___ How important are business goals to you?
___ How important are business achievements to you?
___ How important are business relationships to you?

___ How satisfied are you with your business goals?
___ How satisfied are you with your business achievements?
___ How satisfied are you with your business relationships?

___ How healthy is your current business?
___ How healthy are your business relationships?
___ How healthy are your business goals?

___ Does your business environment inspire you?
___ Does your business environment motivate you?
___ Does your business environment support you?
___ Does your business position you as an expert or authority?
___ Does your business support the legacy you want to leave?

Total Score _____

"Man maintains his balance, poise, and sense of security only as he is moving forward." - Maxwell Maltz

Business & Education Truths

Write down truths about your business and education that would benefit from your attention. These truths do not define you. They are just truths you're willing to face. If you think you got it all together, then you need a reality check. WRITE DAMMIT!

_____

_____

_____

_____

_____

_____

_____

_____

_____

_____

_____

_____

Better to be nobody and yet have a servant than pretend to be somebody and have no food. - Prov 12:9

Business & Education Decision

Turn your relationship truths into life decisions. You wrote about it, now be about it. Write if you're gonna do something about it or give it the finger. I won't tell.

I know…

_____

_____

_____

I want…

_____

_____

_____

I will…

_____

_____

_____

Financial Relationship

Money can warp your world view. It's the biggest measure of success for a lotta folx. You can bee seen as greedy if you charge more than others can afford. You can be seen as cheap choose the best based on price.

On the other side of earning money is spending, saving, and solvency. How you use it after you earn it. Your financial relationship can make you feel some kinda way if you let it define you.

No one can tell you how much money is too much or not enough as a solopreneur. The truth about money is wrapped up in your world view with money. It's a necessary tool to a certain kinda life. You trade it for the life you want. That's the choice you make.

Financial Relationship Evaluation
On a scale of 1-10

___ How important is your financial relationship to you?
___ How important is being generous with others to you?
___ How important are charitable contributions to you?

___ How satisfied are you with your financial relationship?
___ How satisfied are you with your generosity?
___ How satisfied are you with your charity?

___ How healthy are your financial relationship?
___ How healthy are your streams of income?
___ How healthy are your financial goals?

___ You have enough money to meet your needs.
___ You have enough money to meet your wants.
___ You always know what you have in your bank account.
___ You're willing to step out of your comfort zone to generate more income
___ You're willing to take calculated risk to generate new income.

Total Score _____

"A balanced checkbook is not the same as balancing finances when less comes in than goes out." - Phyllis Williams-Strawder

Phyllis Williams-Strawder

Financial Relationship Truths

Write down truths about your financial relationship that would benefit from your attention. These truths do not define you. They are just truths you're willing to face. Funny money is no laughing matter. If nothing else, write about the money you want.

_____
_____
_____
_____
_____
_____
_____
_____
_____
_____
_____
_____
_____
_____

That person is like a tree planted by streams of water, which yields its fruit in season and whose leaf does not wither — whatever they do prospers. - Psa 1:3

Financial Relationship Decision

Turn your financial relationship truths into life decisions. You wrote about it, now be about it. Write if you're gonna do something about it or give it the finger. I won't tell.

I know…

_____

_____

_____

I want…

_____

_____

_____

I will…

_____

_____

_____

Health, Recreation, & Leisure

This right here may seem like a reason to give up your solopreneurship. Health coverage alone will make you run back to a job you hate. When you are financially challenged these may feel like luxuries. They are necessities and they are just for you.

There is no shame in taking advantage of free shit when you need it. Folx try to shame you for it. They will say that's why you need a "real job." Fuck them! You get to decide how to handle this.

One of the most neglected areas of life by the employed and self-employed alike is time for self. Schedule you some down time and get creative with recreation and leisure. Be selfish.

Balance Is Bullshit

Health, Recreation & Leisure Evaluation
On a scale of 1-10

___ How important is your leisure time to you?
___ How important is your physical health to you?
___ How important is your physical activity to you?

___ How satisfied are you with your leisure time?
___ How satisfied are you with your physical health?
___ How satisfied are you with your physical activity?

___ How well do you handle your leisure time?
___ How well do you handle your physical health?
___ How well do you handle your recreational activity?

___ You regularly schedule leisure time.
___ You regularly schedule health checks.
___ You regularly schedule recreational time.
___ How much do you currently enjoy life outside of work
___ How much do you currently enjoy spending time with yourself?
___ How much do you currently dread medical visits?

Total Score _____

"You will never find time for anything. If you want time you must make it." - Charles Buxton

Phyllis Williams-Strawder

Health, Recreation & Leisure Truths

Write down truths about your health, recreation and leisure that would benefit from your attention. These truths do not define you. They are just truths you're willing to face. It's time to get a life. Write about your next trip to the doctor and the vacation you want.

_____

_____

_____

_____

_____

_____

_____

_____

_____

_____

_____

_____

Dear friend, I pray that you may enjoy good health and that all may go well with me, even as my soul is getting along well. - 3 John 1:2

Health, Recreation & Leisure Decision

Turn your health, recreation and leisure truths into life decisions. You wrote about it, now be about it. Write if you're gonna do something about it or give it the finger. I won't tell.

I know...

_____

_____

_____

I want...

_____

_____

_____

I will...

_____

_____

_____

Routine Responsibilities

There is something to be said for doing the same thing, the same way every time. The thing you have to watch out for is turning a routine into a rut. A rut is the boring shit that can cause you to be less productive.

Routines are great for daily habits. Stacked habits can make you feel like you're conquering the world. A rut will have you check crap off the list. And don't get so rooted in routine that you're afraid to try something new.

Routines can have a calming affect that reduces stress. They can easily become cherished traditions or fond memories you share. Make a routine of some of your favorite things so you get joy from them.

Routine Responsibilities Evaluation
On a scale of 1-10

___   How important is managing responsibilities to you?
___   How important is a managing home life to you?
___   How important is managing routine task to you?

___   How satisfied are you with managing responsibilities?
___   How satisfied are you with managing home life?
___   How satisfied are you with managing routine task?

___   You handle managing responsibilities well.
___   You handle managing home life well.
___   You handle managing routine task well.

___   How well do you handle crisis situations?
___   How well do you handle paying routine bills?
___   How well do you handle routine maintenance?
___   How important is it that you have a routine?
___   How important is it that you have flexibility?

                               Total Score _____

"Success is nothing more than a few simple disciplines that are practiced every day." - Jim Rohn

Phyllis Williams-Strawder

Routine Responsibilities Truths

Write down truths about your routine responsibilities that would benefit from some attention. These truths do not define you. They are just truths you're willing to face. Write about the routine you have and how you can make it fun.

_____

_____

_____

_____

_____

_____

_____

_____

_____

_____

_____

_____

_____

_____

A person without self-control is like a city with broken-down walls. - Prov 25:28

Routine Responsibilities Decision

Turn your routine responsibility truths into life decisions. You wrote about it, now be about it. Write if you're gonna do something about it or give it the finger. I won't tell.

I know…

_____

_____

_____

I want…

_____

_____

_____

I will…

_____

_____

_____

Contribution & Giving Back

I could say don't be so fucking stingy, but I don't know if you are. People have the misguided notion that money is the best way to give back. NOT! Time is the most valuable personal commodity you have and where you spend it says a lot.

You could offer someone a job because you've been unemployed. You could give someone a shoulder to cry on because you're familiar with the pain. How you contribute and give back is deeply personal and doesn't need a dollar sign.

The legacy you leave might not get your name on the side of a building or a street corner. But never forget you touch lives every day and that has a ripple effect.

Contribution & Giving Back Evaluation
On a scale of 1-10

___ How important is that you give back?
___ How important is that you leave a meaningful legacy?
___ How important is that you make a difference in the lives of others?

___ How satisfied are you with giving back?
___ How satisfied are you with the current state of your legacy?
___ How satisfied are you with the difference you make in the lives of others?

___ You regularly give back for meaningful impact.
___ You regularly make a positive impact to leave a legacy.
___ You regularly work to make a difference in the lives of others.

___ Those closest to you find value in you.
___ Those you do business with find value in you.
___ You get involved in supporting social issues?
___ You get involved in helping others?
___ You get involved in supporting local issues?

Total Score _____

"Try not to become a person of success but rather try to become a person of value," - Albert Einstein

Phyllis Williams-Strawder

Contribution & Giving Back Truths

Write down truths about your contribution and giving back that would benefit from your attention. These truths do not define you. They are just truths you're willing to face. If you're a selfish ass, own it then write about it. Fa real!

_____

_____

_____

_____

_____

_____

_____

_____

_____

_____

_____

_____

_____

Whoever gives to the poor will lack nothing, but those who close their eyes to poverty will be cursed. - Prov 28:27

Contributing & Giving Back Decision

Turn your contributing and giving back truths into life decisions. You wrote about it, now be about it. Write if you're gonna do something about it or give it the finger. I won't tell.

I know…

_____

_____

_____

I want…

_____

_____

_____

I will…

_____

_____

_____

Mental, Emotional, & Spiritual

Having faith goes a long way in keeping you sane. I'm not talking religion. I'm talking faith. Religion is divisive and my Christian momma would whoop my butt for saying so. Faith, however, is universal and truly defies definition.

Faith is what calms you when shit hits the fan. Your mental and emotional well-being may be tied to your faith. You have faith that doctors know what they're doing. You have faith that love conquers all. You have faith that all things work together for good.

You can't allow yourself to lose faith. You can't ignore your mental and emotional self. Owning these variations of you produce grace and forgiveness when needed. Without faith you wouldn't be a solopreneur.

Mental, Emotional & Spiritual Evaluation
On a scale of 1-10

___ How important is mental health to you?
___ How important is emotional health to you?
___ How important is spiritual health to you?

___ How satisfied are you with your mental health?
___ How satisfied are you with your emotional health?
___ How satisfied are you with your spiritual health?

___ How mentally healthy do you currently feel?
___ How emotionally healthy do you currently feel?
___ How spiritually healthy do you currently feel?

___ Are you confident and secure in who you are as a person?
___ Are you fulfilled in how you currently live your life?
___ Are you content in how you currently live your life?
___ Do you currently invest time in developing yourself mentally, emotionally and spiritually?
___ Do you allow negative emotions get the better of you?

Total Score _____

"A successful man is one who can lay a firm foundation with the bricks others have thrown at him." - *David Brinkley*

Phyllis Williams-Strawder

Mental, Emotional & Spiritual Truths

Write down truths about your mental, emotional and spiritual state that would benefit from your attention. These truths do not define you. They are just truths you're willing to face. It doesn't have to be a fucking journal just write about your state of mind.

_____

_____

_____

_____

_____

_____

_____

_____

_____

_____

_____

_____

_____

_____

...Weeping may endure for a night, but joy comes with the morning. - Psa 30:5

Mental, Emotional & Spiritual Decisions

Turn your mental, emotional and spiritual truths into life decisions. You wrote about it, now be about it. Write if you're gonna do something about it or give it the finger. I won't tell.

I know...

_____

_____

_____

I want...

_____

_____

_____

I will...

_____

_____

_____

- PART III -

Wrap It Up

After reading all this, you may think some kinda way about me. I'm cool with that. I've been rock'n as an entrepreneur, now solopreneur for some years. Your life is your life. Trying to find balance is harder than finding a four leaf clover at the end of the rainbow on a winged unicorn. To experience life is to embrace what comes. You can learn from it or leverage it.

    I enjoy my work. Yes, I would do it without pay if that were possible. I have a family who supports me in my work and how much time I spend on it. Life doesn't get in the way of my work and work doesn't get in the way of my life. While vacationing in Singapore I got on a coaching call at 4am. When we were done, I went back to bed until I woke up for tourist mode. That's a life choice, not a balancing act.

If you're a solopreneur putting in a lot of hours, by choice, baby do yo thang. There are others who are solopreneurs because they wanna spend more time with family. There is no balance required. Just live your best life.

As you live your life you may experience flashes of personal insight or great moments of truth that change the course of your life. Those experiences result from what you would consider your most significant failures, not your successes. And if that's true, then they aren't failures. They're life lessons.

What lessons have you learned from your struggle juggle? To answer the question, ask another question. What happened the last time you said something like, "Damn, I won't do that again." Those are moments of change and transformation.

Life does not require radical choices in order to make significant impact. And not all choices will be easy. Just choose what's sufficient for you to take action in that moment. You choose every morning whether you will face the day or stay in bed. Then you get to choose how you live that day.

I hope reading this far has made you think how you wanna move through life. Writing it made me think about mine and what I will do when I finish it. I'm a big picture thinker and I dream big for those I encounter. I choose to share those big dreams with those who choose to listen. If I drop the ball, who knows what will happen. And the unknown is what we fear most.

Don't let fear keep you from making choices because it might be bad. Unless it's life threatening, whether it's good or bad is arbitrary. After taking action you can decide if it's good or bad.

The evaluations in this book were designed to give you a holistic view of seven important life areas. It's an opportunity to step differently through life. There's a saying that, "The journey of a thousand miles begins with a single step." In case you didn't notice, you're taking steps all day, everyday.

You took your first step as a toddler. You were a fearless baby bad ass. No matter how many times you fell, no matter how many times you cried, you kept getting back up. What about your first day of school and all the steps that came after?

You stepped up for that first kiss. And you stepped into the building of your first job. Now you've stepped into solopreneurship. You've survived a million steps and a million decisions and you're still standing.

Business decisions are still life decisions. It's a new way of juggling. Choose how you want your business to succeed and what you will have to juggle to make it happen. Remember not choosing is still choosing.

My mom had a pretty ordinary life. When she found the lump in her breast, she chose not to go to the doctor. I begged her and still she said no. One day she asked me to do something to make her happy. Since my mom didn't have any hobbies and refused to leave the house anymore, I didn't know what to do so I asked. She couldn't choose anything because she didn't know either.

I respected my mom's choice to ignore what was happening to her body. I chose to do what I could to make her happy. Since she couldn't tell me, I sadly wondered about her list of "if onlys." "If only I'd done things differently... If only I'd made better choices... If only I'd spent more time with..." An "if only" exhaustive list of shoulda, woulda, coulda's. I don't want you to have an "if only" list at the end of your journey.

A life full of indecision is the hallmark of a life lived with "If only's." A list of ifs is for a person who refuses to juggle what's significant to them. Life offers up opportunities for great successes and even more significant lessons describes as failures.

It's up to you to step away from the abyss. In business you make decisions so you can make use of every opportunity that comes your way. If you don't, you run the risk of slowly losing your business and being condemned to a life of mediocrity. Mediocrity is as boring as goldfish water!

The late Stephen Covey said, "Without a clear focus on our guiding values and priorities, each of us runs a real risk of successfully climbing a very long ladder only to find it leaning against the wrong wall." A boring ass wall.

There's safe and there's scared. Don't choose the boring wall out of fear. Don't climb tall ladders for low priorities. The only thing at the top is a note that says "if only." When you look down all you see are the shattered remains of everything you dropped that you wish you hadn't.

Prioritize the decisions you make so you're not doing unnecessary shit. The unnecessary will be there tomorrow. My mom often reminded me that tomorrow's not promised. That didn't keep me from juggling my struggles, dealing with damn distractions, and focusing on flaws. I continued to work on the unnecessary urgencies and ignored the immediately important.

I want you to flip the script and prioritize your decisions before you have to take action. Don't wait for guilt to strike. Be intentional and check in with yourself before you devote time and energy to a **new** pursuit.

You have to see yourself beyond being a solopreneur. You're a person with a life. You can't run a business on empty. Consider your truths and see what area(s) of your life you wanna change today.

Howard Schultz, Starbucks Executive Chairman, said the following about leadership, but I think it can apply to anyone.

> *"Grow with discipline. Balance intuition with rigor. Innovate around the core. Don't embrace the status quo. Find new ways to see. Never expect a silver bullet. Get your hands dirty. Listen with empathy and over-communicate with transparency. Tell your story, refusing to let others define you. Use authentic experiences to inspire. Stick to your values, they are your foundation. Make the tough choices; it's how you execute that counts. Be decisive in times of crisis. Be nimble. Find truth in trials and lessons in mistakes. Be responsible for what you see, hear, and do. Believe."*

Juggling relationships, responsibilities, a business and everything else that goes with it, can get scary. But every time you do something scary, you're less scared. Don't make decisions based on fear. Make decisions based on what you want out of life.

No Pressure

If you're thinking of beating yourself up because you think you should have scored higher in some areas, stop right there. This is not what these evaluations are for. Their only intended use is to open your eyes to some truth. If shit got real and something needs fixing, fix it. If you're okay with it, then be okay with it.

Life is not perfect. Life is not a balancing act. The juggle is real and continuous. Not a means to an end.

If you want something, that doesn't make you a creepy stalker, say you want it. Be specific and intentional about it. Then do what only you can do to make it happen.

If you make a decision for each area of your life and prioritize it for how you wanna live, then you can live life on your terms. If you do nothing then you waste precious time on dreams and regrets.

Put in the hard work of being truthful with yourself. The outcome will be better than you think. Go back and look at how you viewed your life at the beginning of this book. Did the view change?

Whether your feelings changed or not, now you get to choose what action you'll take. Don't accept the premise of same shit different day. You're new every day because something from the day before changed you.

Take your life as it comes and make a decision that works for you and where you are. Stop the struggle and just juggle your shit on your terms without shading others.

Leave yourself a love note of grace:

_____
_____
_____
_____
_____
_____

I hope this was helpful to you because the best life lived, is a life well juggled.

Big smooches sweetheart.

Phyllis

Balance Is Bullshit

Phyllis Williams-Strawder

Other Books By The Author

That Damn Girl Stuff: A Mother's Truth
(Memoir)

Far From The Tree
(Poetry)

About the Author

Phyllis Williams-Strawder is the Founder and HBIC of Brandma's House. She's known as the Ghetto Country Brandmother® who wants to change business failure rate statistics.

Phyllis describes herself as an empathic bitch challenging self-aware solopreneurs who are starting over to use brand strategy to scale their impact as brand leaders. She's here for the respectful rebellion.

Phyllis is a Certified Brand Strategist with additional certifications as a business and life coach. She focuses on being a Brandma to lost brandbabies. She was the business behind the Bigmista brand that is still sought after even though it's been closed for years.

Phyllis is a 20+ year entrepreneur veteran, has a degree in business, is an alum of various executive programs, and always on the hunt for learning something new.

www.ingramcontent.com/pod-product-compliance
Lightning Source LLC
Chambersburg PA
CBHW050528170426
43201CB00013B/2131